Until Life Says No to Me

Until Life Says No to Me

Collected Poems

Margaret Hitchcock

Edited by
Josep Miquel Sobrer

authorHOUSE®

AuthorHouse™
1663 Liberty Drive
Bloomington, IN 47403
www.authorhouse.com
Phone: 1-800-839-8640

Published by AuthorHouse   09/12/2012

ISBN: 978-1-4772-6787-5 (sc)
ISBN: 978-1-4772-6785-1 (e)

Library of Congress Control Number: 2012916839

CONTENTS

Editor's note...ix

1. THINGS, I SAID, THEY'RE JUST THINGS

Listing 3
April Fool.. 5
Sartorial Sequence.. 7
House Cleaner's Song.. 9
The Memory Lingers On 10
My Mother's Voice...11
Mrs. Borton's Bloomers.......................................13
Hair Piece...15
One on One 16
Easy Self-Storage 17
Snapshot...18
Prophet and Loss 19
Scare Tactics 20
Quiet 21
Financial Planning 23
Pray 24
Main Street Nantucket 26
Cézanne's Bather 28
The Setting is Magritte 29
Good Old Days 30

2. A WOMAN WHO EATS THE WHOLE APPLE

Certain Cycle 33
I dream, therefore 34
This Is Just To Say...35
Eating an Artichoke 36

Song to the Senses 37
Mealtime Mayhem 38
Raspberry Recipe... 39
Garlic Love 40
A Little Bit of 41
Live 42
Not Quite Plagiary 43
Followed 44

3. RHYME, REASON, OR THE SNAKE

Untitled 47
The Cage That Words Make 48
Poems 50
Misunderstanding 51
Alphabets 52
Not to Proust 56
Homage to Dorothy Parker...................................... 58
Bedtime Stories 59
The Three Witches 62
Tribe of the Cat 63
PC... 64
A little Advice 65
Citizens.. 66
Fan Letter 67

4. I FEEL THE GROUND BENEATH MY FEET

Seasons 75
Dance: Late September... 76
City 77
See the Sea... 78
Sonnet 79
Raising.. 80
Ghost Scent.. 81
Red Tickets 83

Echo Valley Farm 85
Sleight of Hand.. 87
The Tao 88
Sunday, December.. 89
Already Dated... 90
Three Haiku 91
Old Marrieds.. 92
Global Warning 93
Postcards 95
Trivial Pursuit.. 96
Cedar Camp 98
Spinning... 99
Horizon 100
A long battle... 102

5. THIS SHIFTING LIFE

Essentials.. 107
Princess of Poppycock 110
Glassed-in Porch.. 111
Three Prose Poems.. 112
Ruby Slippers 114
Love, Love, Love... 116
Privileged 117
Fast Fall.. 120
On Acting.. 121
Whensday.. 123
Ambition... 125
Mine 127
9-11 **911 128
Thanksgiving 129
Surprise Compromise 131
Trust... 132
Hug from Hell 133
Generations.. 134

Start.. 135

Travel Lite 136

No extraordinary measures................................. 137

In Progress.. 138

Editor's note

In submitting poems to the journal *Inkwell* in 2003 the poet wrote about herself:

> Margaret Hitchcock was first published in grade 3, in the school magazine; it was a poem about snowdrops written from the point of view of the snowdrop. Since then poetry has had to play second fiddle to motherhood, theater, entrepreneurship, and food writing, but now she finds that the second fiddle plays the most important tune of all.
>
> Margaret Hitchcock lives on Nantucket Island where her work has been published in *Nantucket Writings* and *Post Scripts*. A mother of five, stepmother to five more, and now acquiring descendants at a steady rate, she has been at various times the founder/owner of a health foods store and bakery, an actor, a food writer, and always a traveler and a poet.

Margaret Hitchcock died in 2009 before she was able to gather her poems in a volume. She left them printed on sheets or paper and some saved only on her computer. With the help of her daughters Francesca Sobrer and Gillian Lewis, after the rest of the family kindly agreed to name me Margaret's literary executor, I was able to put together all the poems that have survived.

The 93 poems I have been able to gather, furthermore, arrived to me without any indication as to date of composition or the intention of the author to present them in any given order. I have decided to divide the whole of Margaret Hitchcock's production into five sections according to the main themes found in her poems. I have given each section a title taken from one of the poems therein, and I have also used one of her lines for the title of the collection. Her subject matters include everyday objects (section 1: 'Things, I said, they're just things'), food (2. 'A woman who eats the whole apple'), word-play and literature (3. 'Rhyme, reason, or the snake'), places—including her beloved Nantucket—and seasons (4. 'I feel the ground beneath my feet'), and the times of one's existence (5. 'This shifting life').

As editor I have regularized punctuation and capitalization and corrected only obvious misspellings. I have also unified the fonts found in the typescripts and files, but have respected the author's choice to print her verses with a flush left margin or across a central axis.

Acknowledgements are due to: *Amherst Review* ("April Fool" 2003), *Prairie Winds* ("Bedtime Stories" 2004), *Southern Poetry Review* ("Cézanne's Bather" 2004), *Nantucket Magazine* ("Ghost Scent" 2003), *Inkwell* ("My Mother's Voice" 2003), *Chrysalis Reader* ("The Setting is Magritte" 2004), *Carquinez Poetry Review* ("This is Just to Say" 2005), *Confrontation* ("Sonnet" 2006).

Josep Miquel Sobrer
Bloomington, Indiana, summer of 2012

1.

THINGS, I SAID,
THEY'RE JUST THINGS

Listing

I could not sleep,
or cry, or think,
or dream.
I could only list
and in my
listing
grasp the objects
around me.
The rough wood table,
the pile of magazines,
jars of pencils
and pens,
the teacup
and spoon.
The blue and white
china rabbit.
Seashells and stones.
Recipes
all stained
with oil
and flour.
The dusty bunch
of dried flowers.

Tomorrow's cake,
one pan with
cat tracks
across the surface.
Listing badly
in this detritus,
which object
provided the life raft?
The saving grace?
Flour, flowers,
seashells, stones?
Maybe the jar of
pens and pencils?
Or was it all
these things
that floated me
back to shore?
Brought back
the tears,
the thought,
the sleep,
the dreams.

MARGARET HITCHCOCK

April Fool

Lately, I have been dropping things.
Not exactly dropping them;
they seem to slip away
and crash.

The brand new coral café-au-lait bowl,
the platter from Portugal,
a gift from Gillian.

The creamer to the Limoges tea set,
Sèvres it said on one shard,
severed, at any rate, no longer useful.

The handle to "A fine kettle o' fish"
teapot from the British Design Institute,
the pottery pun I gloried in.

Things, I said, they're just things.
Then, slithering through my fingers
crashing to the floor
the last blue glass with yellow stars
but one.

Just the same I'll keep away
from the bowl from Avebury.
The one that says in tiny print,
hand-done on the bottom,
"For the joy of the good green earth."

I'm not touching it just now
I won't look to see.
Not while this dropping disease
Is afflicting me.
That bowl is one of a kind:
Avebury, p. D.,
that's Avebury pre-Disneyfied.

If the only way to keep
the joy of the good green earth
is on the bottom of a bowl
on a shelf,
so be it.

MARGARET HITCHCOCK

Sartorial Sequence

1

I had nothing up my sleeve.
No ace of hearts
no fall-back plan.
My sleeve was
loose and silken,
too open and soft
to hide anything.

But you, you with your
perfect sleeve for
hiding things
held all the aces
and a long string
of silken, many colored scarves
with a little dagger
at the end.

2

You better believe
I wore tight sleeves
after that.

But they held no tricks
and were confining.
So I began to
push them up
just a little.

The scar showed then
but with light and air
it began to fade
into a little comma,
a small illustration
on my skin map.

3

Now I go sleeveless
and there is more
than one comma
on my skin.
But, oh, the
many colored scarves
I have seen.

House Cleaner's Song

They have pictures, signs
all over the house.

LOVE, they say. Some
with cats, some

with geraniums:
LOVE.

It makes me a little
bit nervous.

Are they reminding
themselves?

Or do they hang
it on the wall

to keep love in its place,
out of their way?

The Memory Lingers On

I sought to hold
the memory of you

like a scene in
an Easter egg.

A small perfect world
bright, concise, and hidden.

I thought to return
there, whenever I

most needed to.
That moment in

time. Safe inside
the Easter egg.

When did it fade,
turn into a bouquet

of dried flowers
lovely, but scentless

without the fresh green
a ghost of a scene.

MARGARET HITCHCOCK

My Mother's Voice

1

A voice like foghorns,
like train whistles
in the night,
The faint
far-off rumble
of the train
on the tracks,

A rough command
a deep caress
a voice loved
by babies
and men.

2

The coat hangs on its hook
the rough gray wool
in stiff folds.
The pockets permanently
poked outward
from carrying
a trowel, a pair of snips.

If you thrust your hand
into them
you will find a few
errant, outdated seeds,

a dried blade
of grass
or two,
a neatly folded tissue.

I can hear
her say
"Those damned deer
they eat everything.
The lawn needs mowing
again.
Your father loves to
plant things
but I'm the one
who weeds them."

Outside, the lawn
has returned to meadow.
The flowers the deer
have not eaten
have escaped their border
and grow
anywhere they please
side by side
with weeds.

The old order is gone,
the old coat hangs on.

MARGARET HITCHCOCK

Mrs. Borton's Bloomers

Mrs. Borton's bloomers
hang from the thin wire

crossing the porch ceiling
of swimming-pool blue.

Made of mauve chintz
with beige hydrangea blossoms

outlined in black
they hang from the wire.

Black snakeskin, spike heeled
boots hang from the wire.

A sharp contrast to the
billowing bloomers of Mrs. B.

Wake up, you're dreaming.

The shushususuring of the swing
on the porch lulls the senses.

For contrast I put a red and yellow
parrot on a perch, on the porch

with the turquoise ceiling
the boots and bloomers
of Mrs. B.

Wake-up, you're dreaming.

Hair Piece

Damn, I've got good hair.
It's been gold, it's been red, and it's been brown.
It's been short, it's been long, it's been up, it's been down.
It's been curled, it's been straight, every which way.
I've reason to think it's soon going to be gray.
Or maybe white, or maybe blue,
it seems to welcome every hue.
Babies have swung from it
men have drowned in it.

It's the only part of me
that won't succumb to gravity.
Damn, I've got good hair.

One on One

As I tossed
the magazine
aside an ad
"China for Two,"
caught my eye.

As I drifted
off
I wondered:
was it
a starter set
of porcelain
or
entwined tickets
to the Orient?

Being one,
I let it go
and went
to sleep.

Easy Self-Storage

Phone's off the hook,
curtains are drawn.
I lie in bed.
Nothing is on.
Not the TV, the
radio or the computer;
Certainly not me.

I'm not coming out.
Not to work or to play.
I'm here in self storage
for an indefinite stay.

Snapshot

There I am
a small, slightly chubby
kid under an avalanche
of hair, holding the
tail of a rattlesnake,
a dead rattlesnake.

You cannot see the
paper towel between
hand and snake.
What you can see
is how far away
I stand from that snake.

There is another little
girl on the other side.
She is helping to
hold the snake.
It is almost
as long as
we are tall and
wears an amazing
diamond pattern
on its back.

Prophet and Loss

We make ourselves ill
with our toys,
with our necessities
as well.
We watch screens
that tell us
we need, need, need.
This, that, them.

We no longer sing
our own songs.
No longer dance
our own dance.
If we ever did
it is hard to remember.

If you are able, please come
sing your own song,
dance your own dance.
If we can remember
there may still be time.

Scare Tactics

Be afraid, be afraid, be afraid.
Kill the enemy.
If you haven't any
make one up.

There are many
to choose from;
terrorists, anarchists,
smokers, jokers.

Be afraid of the
future, our future,
our dying planet,
our obesity and bad breath.

Think poor, think need,
think SUV, think bling.
Do not think of the cost;
the unseen backs of those

who made them possible.
Those whose backs they
came from. Those who have
barely enough, or less.

Stay in the now
with what you have.
Don't question the power
that you gave away.

Margaret Hitchcock

Quiet

Silence, I shouted,
    SILENCE.
I don't want to hear
    anymore.

And my wish
was granted.
I stood alone
outside the door
of the world.

In silence so profound
I could not remember
the world of sound.

No yelling, no sirens,
no crashing of bombs.

No bees buzzing in
the mulberry bush.

No laughter filling
frilled happy ears.

No screams, no music
no weeping, no tender sighs.

Silence is golden
someone said
but I tell you,
it is more like lead.

Financial Planning

I say "hare" to the listening air
and quickly douse
the light.

Morning light comes,
slides open my eyes:
"rabbit" is what
I mutter.

Hare and Rabbit
my personal
bull and bear.

Hare the last
thing at the
end of the month,

Rabbit the first
word on the
first day of
the month.

If these rules you carefully heed
for that month you'll have what you need.

Pray

History teaches us
not one thing.

Not one single thing.
History is as selective

as memory. Every bit
as deceptive.

If we really remembered
Hitler and Hiroshima . . . and

somewhere, someone must.
The terrible cost

of all that power
given to our leaders,

I would not be
sitting here, watching

first Saddam, and
then George W

in despair, trying
to comfort myself

by imagining their
underwear.

Cotton boxers from
L.L. Bean for George,
silk briefs from
Paris for Saddam.

What is that phrase
about power corrupts?

Ah, yes, absolute
power corrupts
absolutely.

Main Street Nantucket

SUVs lumber
across cobblestones
tapped here securely

over a hundred years ago
by skillful hands using
ballast from the tall ships.

Smooth stones driven deeper
each year. First by rolling
wagons, carriages, horse's hooves

followed by the hard
rubber of the Model T.
and always the feet

shod in boot, clog,
dainty slipper, and later
sandal, spike heel, flip-flop.

Worn first by force
of water, then by
traffic weight, settled

into earth. Survivor of
ice, fire and storm,
mute testaments to time.

The porpoise waltzes held
on long, dark winter nights
are just one of their secrets.

Cézanne's Bather

There he stands,
the reluctant
risk-taker,
elbows akimbo,
sharp and wary,
his mouth a moue
of doubt.

Yet his large
strong feet
carry him
to the water,
hot or cold
or
just right.
He doesn't
know.

Elbows hold
back,
feet carry
forward,
So.

The Setting is Magritte

Five a.m.
There is a rectangle of
moonlight on the floor
halfway to the bathroom.
The sky is that pale
blue-green, more green
really.

Mr. A's house across the way
has a square of light
in the kitchen window.
He is old
and wakes early.

The setting is Magritte.
Any moment now a man
wearing a derby
carrying an open
umbrella
will float through
the back leaves.

I look so long
I do not see the
hooded figure enter.

Early mornings now,
the window is
no longer lit.

Good Old Days

I'm tired of perfection.
The shiny, impervious paint
on every house and face;
seamless, timeless, soulless.

I want the old houses back.
The ones with time on them,
cracked, wrinkled, settled in
full of stories.

The place that wears the
fog like a shawl.
The face that wears a
wonderful story.

Erase time's traces:
Erase the soul.

2.

A WOMAN WHO EATS
THE WHOLE APPLE

Certain Cycle

Out of the seed, the shoot.
Out of the shoot, the flower.
Out of the flower, the fruit.

Which contains the seed
which contains the shoot
which contains the flower
that foretells the fruit.

I dream, therefore . . .

I am the color of the evening sky
after the sun has set when the
first evening star has appeared
perhaps a crescent moon.

I am the color of moss: soft,
deep. The color of new
leaves opening and grass.
I am the ocean.

I am the color of the sun,
the sunset, and
the sunrise. I am
sky always, and

water; clear, muddy,
and I am the smell
of water and the
sound of water too.

I am a bowl of cherries,
the dark red kind
also the yellow ones
flecked with rose.

I am cherry juice
and the purple twilight
of mountains seen
from far away.

MARGARET HITCHCOCK

This Is Just To Say

I'm sorry you don't know what to do
with a woman who eats the whole apple.
I would love to show you how to savor
each almond-bitter seed,
to pleasure in the contrast
of red and white,
slippery and firm. The juice
running down your chin.
But I can see that you
want to peel the apple
core it and slice it, eat
only the part guaranteed to be safe.

Eating an Artichoke

The way that artichokes
are peeled off
leaf by leaf.
Each tender tip
dipped in butter
and pulled through
the teeth
one by one.

Then the heart
hidden in protective
prickly choke.
Remove the choke,
dip the heart
in butter.
Savor the sweet
aftertaste.

Song to the Senses

There is nothing like
the feel of bare feet
on a warm dirt road
unless it is the feel
of a friend's hand
held in yours
as you walk
down the road.

There is nothing like bare
feet crossing slippery
rock and smooth moss
unless it is sitting
in the brook,
a small cascade
of crystal water
over each shoulder.

Unless you've brought a jar
of ripe black olives to share.
Now you're there.
Nothing like it.

Mealtime Mayhem

I riced it, diced it,
beat, and whipped it,

pound it, ground it,
sliced, and chopped it.

When I had my food
subdued
I ate it.

Raspberry Recipe

Find the bush
then the berry.
place it in
your mouth
full of sun.
Crush with tongue.
Lush.

Garlic Love

Some compare their
love to roses
or lilies.

But my love
is like
firm white garlic.

Sharp, sweet, distinct,
yet blending
with many things.

Adaptable, but never
assimilated
and taste that lingers on.

Come with me,
my garlic love.
We will many

dishes make.
I will never tire
of your variety.

A Little Bit of . . .

Nothing is better
than butter.

A little bit of
butter for my
bread, peas,
pancakes, and teatime

scones, not to
mention asparagus,
fish, baked potato,
cloverleaf roll, and
corn on the cob.

I don't disdain
olive oil; it's good,
but not a butter
substitute at all.

As for oleo,
oh, well, that is
just culinary hell.

Nothing is better
than butter.

Live

You cannot live without food, water, shelter.
You cannot live without love.
You cannot survive without food, water, shelter.
You can survive without love.

How good it is then that
you don't have to live without love.
Because love is in you, with you
always there for the taking.

While food and shelter must be
found, love is always there.
Folded in the batter of
your making, a dash of love.

Some of us don't know the
secret ingredient and survive,
but do not live.
No living without love.

Not Quite Plagiary

"You are the bread and the knife.
You are the crystal goblet and the wine"

You are my necessity.
I am lost without you.

I sit here with muffin and spoon,
coffee, in a paper cup.

Where are you, my bread,
My knife, my oh so necessary life.

I raise my cup to the tinsel moon
hoping you will get here soon.

My crystal goblet filled with wine,
my one and only Valentine.

Whoever you are, I wait for you.
Until you come I'll just make do

with my muffin and spoon and
a sip of coffee in a paper cup.

Followed

The crescent moon
follows me home
and hangs itself
over the white
bloom of the
pear tree.

3.

RHYME, REASON, OR THE SNAKE

Untitled

Poetry is
an arrangement,
an accident
of words
that convey, say,
the moon gliding,
sliding, hiding
among the
clouds,
any extraordinary
ordinary event.

Sounds released
to please or pluck
the ear strings,
the heart strings,
the mind's eye
watching the moon
gliding, sliding by.

The Cage That Words Make

Come, put your hand
in the hornet's nest,
the leader says
to me, to us, to them.

In the name of freedom,
patriotism
    honor.

Freedom is a word
and honor too.

No one mentions
fear, or love;
more operative, here.

The real words:
oh shit, oh hell,
oh God.

Even they clink
like lead
in a gun barrel.

What about
power, now
there's a dangerous
word.

One it seems, that
can be heard.

Over love and fear
freedom and joy.

Power's such a pretty toy
must have it now.

Poems

Sometimes they arrive
like an attack,
a flood of words
dictated from on high
or the gut, who knows,
and those you put
away and in a day
or two read them
and blush, or say
possibly, with a little
work, or even
not too bad.
Then there are the
ones that got away.
Turned into dust bunnies
under the bed,
or sitting like a
kitten in a tree;
and the fire department
won't come.
Those that tease,
give you a phrase
then go away
or are perverse
presenting the last
verse first.
It seems the trick is
to let them through
and then tell the
words what to do.

Misunderstanding

I shot a word (or two) into the air.
It landed, I know exactly where.
Can it be true, is that, my love,
my word sticking out of you?
Is that the word I so lately shot?
No, my dear, it's definitely not.
The word (or two) I recently let fly
has landed in a different guise.
For what I said
and what you heard
there ought to be another word.

Alphabets

One

After being a coward
Doing effectively fuck-all,
George had had it.
Jumped his Karma,
leapt many miles
not noticing
open places
quite quiet
restful serene
tumescent
under veils
of water
extending
from
zero to zero.

Two

Apples are better
cold.
Delicious, Eve
furnished
and Granny Smith.

Held in her hand
icily inviting.
Jumping knowledge
Leaping man
new and needing nurture
openly prideful
questioned not
rhyme, reason
or the snake.
Took umbrage
had visions.
Wanting, wanting, wanting
exploding
youth's zenith.

Three

Always be
cool, calm, collected
don't ever forget
grinning, gasping, glorying
have instantaneous
jarring, killing
libelous, mortifying, nasty
often
perilous, queer results.

So stay serene,
try underplaying.
Voicing vainly
will exacerbate
a young
zealot's zeitgeist.

Four

Art
becomes
culture
discovers
ever
finer
grades of
happiness, hell, and heaven
instead
joins
kitsch and
life.
Maybe, maybe
not
of
poetry's

queer
reality
so thinks
us
victims
we, wee, whee
exit in
yawns of
zappiness.

Not to Proust

I cannot read Proust.
Ten pages in and
I am transported
back to my childhood
bedroom; staring into space
seeing the mottled beige
walls, the blue rug
the child size table
and chairs, the bureau
painted ivory, a small
parade of blue ducks
crossing the largest
drawer. On top
a small hair brush,
a bureau scarf, white linen
edged in crochet, a china
dish for pins,
a cardboard card
on which is written
"The meek shall inherit the earth."
Why should they get it,
I wonder. Thinking the meek
are the people of Meece or
Meecedonia, something like that.
I thought the earth
was everyone's forever.

Long since disabused of that
I still don't think
it fair; consider meekness
then the word inherit, which seems
far enough away to say
the hell with it
(meekness, that is).
Minutes have passed and
I am returned to my present
room. Proust in my lap,
my personal madeleine that
I cannot consume but only
nibble round the edges
remembering times past.

Homage to Dorothy Parker

This is just to say
I love you anyway.
Why I do, I have no clue
but I love you anyway.

Love you enough to open
the door and send you
into the arms of your
new lover, anyway.

It's very clear and a little queer
that I should feel this way.
I love you enough to
give you up. I will
go and try my luck
elsewhere, anyway.

Bedtime Stories

There are those times
when counting sheep
is not enough,

when somehow
it leads
to Bo-peep.

Those sheep
wagging their tails
behind them.

From there
to the three
little piggies

whose name is
one vowel removed
from being the
same as mine

as a child.
I identified.
Imagined the

big, bad wolf
lurking in
the dark.

Waiting to
huff and puff
my fragile
house down.

Or to be swallowed
whole by that
other wicked wolf
the one that ate Grandma.

Which leads somehow
to Cinderella,
who got her fella.
Was she really
happy ever after?

Or did she get
bored with
waving her
little white glove
and having
everything done
for her?

Did she tire
of princess life
and turn into
Eleanor Roosevelt?

By now I am
ready for
a bite of
the apple

that the wicked
queen gave
to Snow White.
Ready to
be enveloped
in a cloak
of dreams

which will be
unwrapped
by the kiss
of morning
if not the
handsome prince.

The Three Witches

Big bad words.
Blame, guilt, shame.
Evil trio of fate.

Light and love shine
down and forth,
in and out, polish,

scour away fear,
doubt, all dread.
That peace, not pain
may reign instead.

Tribe of the Cat

The girls with the celadon eyes
sit round the table
candlelit from below
laughter and tears
tremble and shine
in candle glow.

Girls of the tribe of the cat
with celadon eyes
celadon, celadon, celadon eyes.
Work the magic spell
they do so well.
To others it's a
surprise
but not to the girls with the
celadon, celadon, celadon eyes.

Anyone comes in this circle
after time and time again
comes into tears and laughter
comes into time before
when the tribe of the cat
became women.
Felicitous, feline girls.
No paws or twitching tail
to betray them
only their
celadon, celadon, celadon eyes.

PC

People of color,
that's everyone
except of course
the colorless.

The hope
one day,
to all be
colorful.

A little Advice

Jane has lovely eyes you say,
dark as night and warm as day.
Well, my dear, I quite agree,
but go tell Jane,
don't tell me.

Diane is graceful as a gazelle.
Yes, my dear, I know that well.
Tell Diane about her grace,
go and tell her to her face.
I am not the one to tell.

Mabel's witty, Sally's pretty,
Laura's legs are long and lovely.
So I see,
but don't tell me.

My eyelashes are dark and long,
my rounded arms are very strong,
my smile can melt at fifty paces.
Don't tell Diane, Jane, or Sally
about my many graces.
Get smart, sweetheart:
tell me.

Citizens

"citizens gathered to protest the violence, throwing rocks at the police"
NPR news; Sunday, March 3, 2007

Peace. Is it simply
non-violence or
is it more?
King, Gandhi, Buddha, Jesus,
were they Princes of Peace
or simply non-violent?
No, they were actively
peaceful.
Without throwing rocks.

Fan Letter

Dear Billy Collins, I am
in love with you.
Or the you I find
in your poetry.
The man who splits
wood, hears jazz,
and has a dog.
Who gives equal
attention to sausages
and jealousy,
who was a boy
on a trike
riding in circles.

One of the first
boys I ever knew
was called Billy,
Billy Aiken, I
used to go to
his house and
play trains.
He wouldn't let
me touch them
which was a little boring,
but he did allow me
to tell him what I
wanted them to do.

I was smart enough
not to ask for
a crash, though if
I had ever been left
alone with them
that was the first
thing I would have
tried to do.
Billy's mother gave
us milk and cookies,
those dry no-taste cookies
and I have never liked milk.

There was another boy
I played with.
His name was Jimtee,
Jimtee McCall.
He had red gold hair,
sparkling brown eyes,
and rosy cheeks.
With Jimtee I played
house. Under the card
table covered with a
large table cloth that
came to the floor,

We would go to bed,
lie rigid as corpses
on the living room floor.
Side by side, until
I would rise and say
"Time to get up, darling"
and Jimtee would get
up and shave, while
I put on the coffee.

After breakfast he
would kiss me
on the cheek
and crawl out
from underneath
the tablecloth
while I stayed
home to tidy up
and get dinner
ready. This took
about five minutes
and then Jimtee
would return, calling
"I'm home, dear" and crawling
under the tablecloth
would kiss me
on the cheek.

Then we would dine
and I made him
eat his peas
before he got
dessert. He
would tell me
about his day
and then we
would lie down
side by side,
effigies on a tomb
after a kiss goodnight.
Jimtee's mother didn't
serve cookies and milk,
but there was a
candy dish on the
coffee table and when
we got tired of air
we would eat the kisses
and butterscotch that
were there.
I don't know, Billy,
maybe it's just your
name. You haven't
turned into Willy or
William or Bill.

Then again, I get the
idea from your poems
that you would have
let me touch your train,
crash it even.
That your mother
would have served
homemade cookies
and ginger ale.
That you
would have known
how to lie, like
two spoons in a box.

I made this last up.

But this much is true:
you have returned me
to an innocence
I once knew.
Dear Billy Collins,
I love you.

4.

I FEEL THE GROUND
BENEATH MY FEET

Seasons

Spring hovers at the entrance
unsure of her lines.

Summer zooms past her
taking center stage.

'Til fall with perfect timing
steals the show.

Then winter comes and stays
on stage too long.

And once again
frail spring
is in the wings.

Dance: Late September

Still green leaves
twitching to
an invisible breath
of cool air
waiting
to give up
their summer color.
A wet warm summer
that made
an emerald isle
of this
gray lady
now . . . tentatively
lifting her
petticoats
to show a brief
flash
of gold or red.
The trees impatient
to fling off
their leaves
and dance bare and gaunt
once again.
Heavy, dusty, green
heads nodding,
feet tapping,
they wait for
the shivery blast
to bring them
flame, fire, and ash.

City

Gazing down the
man-made canyons,
watching the
buttoned down,
buttoned up,
sewn in their skins,
people
dashing by.
I feel the ground
beneath my feet
tremble.
Interlaced with
pipes and wires,
subways and sewers,
so much spaghetti
down there.

And yet,

like a tendril
escaping from
a spinster's bun,
a stranger's smile
reminds me
what an act of faith
the city is.

See the Sea

Here's the summer sea
flipping her frilled petticoats
over the supine beach.
Twinkling her diamonds
rolling over slowly
to reveal
voluptuous blue-green depths.

The same salt sea
that swallows ships whole
and spits back the
garbage we toss into her.

Listen.
You think that's
sigh, slap,
sigh, sigh, slap?
No, oh no, those sibilants
hiss and roll
here then, here now.
Here when
you're gone.
hear, here, here.

Sonnet

Don't you want to go to heaven?
I asked my mother. She didn't
pause for a second. No, she said,
none of my friends will be there.
And I, aged only six or seven,
saw no other choice. Hell or Heaven.
Ma wanted to go down below?
Fire and brimstone and all that?
Now, when I plant seeds
and they don't do well
I imagine them flowering
on the ceilings of hell.
    Look up, dear mother, look and see,
      Enjoy the garden sent from me.

Raising

I am having trouble trusting
the miracle of seed into plant,
trusting myself as a gardener.
Have I got the soil fine enough?
Will the weeds stay weeded?

And then the wait.
I pretend not to care,
and then
the miracle of miracles:
a plant rises there.

Will I be able to grow it up
keep it from rabbits, deer,
bugs, and drought?
Keep it safe until
it will flourish?

If I can,
it will nourish me.

Ghost Scent

When the privet blooms in Nantucket
the whole island smells heady, sweet
like a bathroom recently vacated
by a hormone hounded teenager.

In this time of privet bloom
flowers press against window
boxes and picket fences
struggling to get free.

The heavy headed hydrangeas
create false seas of blue
all along the foundations
of the prim, gray houses.

Along the one-way streets,
befuddled bikers ride the wrong way,
while poor, privileged prisoners in
air-conditioned SUVs struggle
to avoid them.

The ghosts of sea captains,
whalers, farmers, and fishermen,
and the enterprising ladies
who stayed home and minded
the store, gather on the steps

of the Pacific Bank and sing
faint sea chanteys which
the living mistake for nocturnal
birds or distant thunder.

The ghosts are no longer
at home in their former
mansions, cottages, shacks,
all of which have been
renovated, redone, updated,
changed beyond recognition
to fit the new idea of old.

Poor ghosts. They wander
from place to place looking
for themselves, only to find
new ghosts in the making.

The scent of privet, tempered
by salt from mud flats at
low tide, still wends its way
through the smell of exhaust
and binds them here.

Red Tickets

'Twas the night before Christmas.
Down in the street
thousands of people
were stamping their feet.
Bob gave me his, and Mary, and Jane,
and with my own I'd a chance of a claim.
My bottom was resting
on a stone step so cold
but thoughts of big dollars
made me quite bold.
The children were gazing
about with much glee
hoping to hear Santa
talk out of the tree.
I thought I had many chances
but, look, over there
they have so many
they must have spent every penny.
The Town Criers bell began ringing,
the Choir ceased singing,
a visible hush fell over the crowd.
Who has the red ticket,
the winning red ticket?
When will they pick it
out of the hat?

One thousand, two thousand, five thousand, three,
oh, let there be a red ticket for me.
The numbers were called.
None of them mine.
Maybe I'll have better luck
next time.
So off to the houses
the people all went.
A few lucky ones
were glad of the money they spent.
But most were thinking
as they lay down their head:
I've spent so much money
I should have stayed in my bed.

May your Christmas be merry, may your Christmas be wise.
Keep your eye on the sentiment, not on the prize.

Echo Valley Farm

If you were to unwrap
my heart, unwind the long
ribbon of beloved faces and
places, you would find at
the center, this place.

A child's drawing where
hill meets hill. In the
valley sits a square white
house with porch, door
in center, a window at
either side, and three above.

A small well-house sits
under the sentinel maple
on the goose-dotted lawn
that lies between house and
dusty red dirt road.

Across road and a field
lies a brook that sings
in springtime and sighs
in summer. My special toy,
deep dreaming in summer,
silver fish in spring, ice in winter.

Behind the house lies
a small cottage of lilac bushes,
my hiding place and secret den.
On a rise an apple tree goes
from pink cloud to green

to odd shaped yellow apples
to bare armature, ready
to have ice and snow applied.
This huge small place
in the eye of my heart.

Sleight of Hand

Starlight littered the
farmhouse lawn.

The children chase
it with small jars.

Captured and kept it,
watched by the

undiminished stars
burning overhead.

The Tao

Soon I will awake,
rise like a

brilliant afterthought
from my bed

of milkweed, shake out
elegant, orange wings

and, amid a shower
of thistledown,

sip from a late
flower. And begin

my long journey
to another hemisphere.

MARGARET HITCHCOCK

Sunday, December

Wakened from sleep
by raucous clamor
of geese.

They vee-ed across
the north window
then the east
making their noisy way south.

Snow fell quietly
as they flew.

Snow falling
Geese flying
no need
for church
today.

Already Dated

Hurray, hurrah for the first
of May in this the year of our Lord 2003.

Is this a year of our Lord? Must be.
No one says that anymore. Do they?

Right now, this minute, some starlings
sit in a maple sapling, that just

minutes ago, it seems, was a weed
I should have pulled, but now

strong enough to hold four starlings
that the wind, or their will has

blown away. In the distant past of
an hour or so, a crow ate something

on the roof across the way, while
I breathed in blue to strengthen my bones.

Margaret Hitchcock

Three Haiku

In gray of winter
cardinal threads his scarlet
through the thin black trees.

Hieroglyphics of gull feet
mysterious marks
stamped on wet sand.

Crescent moon follows me
home, settles over where
bloom of pear tree.

Old Marrieds

The cardinal and his wife
come in late afternoon
to stitch-tsk in
the quince tree.

Their conference is short
a flash of red, a rosy brown
against the ripening
yellow quince.

Where are the children?
Stitch-tsk, stitch-tsk.
Did the jay dispossess
them again this year?

Or are these the children?
No, the way they talk
They must be a pair.
A brief conversation,

an early supper
in the quince.
Stitch-tsk, stitch-tsk.
Red and gold and rosy brown.

Global Warning

Big fat flakes float
and whirl about.
Is there someone
inside the house
with the light
streaming out?
The little house
in the snow
with a flagstone
path, a hedge, and
a tree, and yes
I think that must
be me.

Over here is
a child with
tongue stuck out
to catch the flakes.

Way over there
the soldier with the vacant stare,
the homeless man in cardboard shelter,
the statue in the empty square.

Big fat flakes float
around us all.
The same hand shakes the globe
and makes the snowflakes whirl
on all of us, or
drops the globe
and all of us.

MARGARET HITCHCOCK

Postcards

Paris

It stays light late in Paris.
We eat crepes
in the crepuscule.
There is no sunset.
Wish you were here.

Madrid

The air is dry,
blue blue sky
very Spanish
red and yellow
outlined in black.
You were here, I wish.

Scotland

It rains and rains.
My room is cold,
a gale blows
through the lounge.
I'm going to the pub.
Wish I was there.

Trivial Pursuit

Already my waking mind is burying
my dreams
shoving them aside for the details
of the day.
Breakfast and a brief read will do that.

Still I want to remember.

I was held in someone's arms
persistently, closely, fondly.
And while it was somehow
pleasurable
in another way I felt
trapped.
Tried to unpry myself
saying all the while
"Let me go, let me go."

Wake briefly to find
myself holding myself.

Back to sleep to wake
into a dream of
being in bed in a room
with a wide window wall
overlooking a lake.

A dark green lake
with miraculous birds,
beige and gold and pale blue,
swimming and strutting
in elegant pairs.

On the white beach
are other small animals.
dogs I think, why yes,
delicious, red-gold
friendly dogs.
A gray cat appears
at the edge of the scene.

I leave that dream
to go on to one in which
I attend a diplomatic party
where I do not
know the rules
and everyone ignores me.

Now I light a cigarette,
blow the dreams away.
I have friends coming
for lunch and
the house is a mess.

Cedar Camp

The harbor is wearing
her very best
ultramarine dress.

The one with the
white lace
    collar.

Her gold necklace
of rushes glints
    in the sun.

A single sail
brooches her
dark bosom.

A swift moment
of peace.

Spinning

In the evening
a big yellow moon
rose in the east,

rolled across the
sky all night
turning silver
as it went.

The moon spun west
while the earth turned
toward the sun.
Sun in east, moon in west.

I lie still, in bed
on the spinning earth
pinned by gravity.

I am so safe,
warm and still,
wedged between
the sun and the moon.

Night and day
visible and whole.
Yet I know
I am spinning too.

Horizon

We sit on the sand,
the old dog and I.
I lean on a rock,
she leans on me.
We gaze at the sea.
We are
deeply content.

Soon we will rise
and walk slowly
on the firm
wet sand
at the edge
of the water.
Our bare soles
will feast
on every nuance
of damp sand.
Her still-sharp nose
will query
the surrounding air.
My dimming gaze
will look
to the horizon.

Someday we will
stand still
and our footprints
will go on
ahead of us.
We will be
deeply content.

A long battle

We sit here
unlikely warriors,
some brave in caps and hats,
others with hair.

Some have spouses,
one wife with
shaking hands
unwraps a sandwich

for her husband.
We are all
attached to IVs,
one of the weapons

for this battle.
Overhead dance
a thousand
bright paper cranes,

those origami symbols
of prayer, of hope.

These people with their
waxen, hollow faces
look like saints and martyrs
in an old master, or

a supplicant crowd
gathered beneath the cross,
guests at some peculiar
Last Supper.

There are no
children here.
There is a special
room for them.

That is a blessing,
because everyone here
would gladly give
their remaining years
to them. The children,
and that would be
giving up the battle.

5.

THIS SHIFTING LIFE

Essentials

at nine

A book.
Fuzzy, my Teddy bear.
Sunday silk underwear.

at fourteen

A book.
The appearance
of sophistication.
A stash of Milky Ways.

at nineteen, then

A book.
A come hither look.
Travel, trouble.
A decision.

at twenty-four

A book.
Little time
to read.
Love out-flowing.

at twenty-nine

Four babies,
One divorce, no time
for a book.

at thirty-four

A book.
With children now
numbering ten.
Books an escape
now and then.

at thirty-nine

A book
You know she
can't hear you
when she's reading.

at forty-nine

A book
Explanation time
How-to, say
no
and mean it.

at fifty-nine

A book
Back to school
learn the lines
Chekhov, Shakespeare
now are mine.

at sixty-nine

A book
To read, learn
and/or for
escape.
A book to write.

Princess of Poppycock

I am the practically
perfect princess of
poppycock.

Pretty and playful
not quite practical
or perfect.

You may address me
as your highness
or lowness or slowness

or your plumpness
maybe—Her Peachiness
o simply, Princess.

Glassed-in Porch

When the air grew chill,
days short and bright,
my grandmother put
up a small glass
room on the front porch.
She banked it on every side
with pots and pots
of chrysanthemums.

We would have tea
there in the long
late-afternoon light.
The scent of
chrysanthemums
would envelop us.

To be there was
to be a bee, sipping tea
inside a chrysanthemum.

Now, it seems, chrysanthemums
smell of death
and football games.
But I can *see* that room.
I am a bee, inside the
chrysanthemum.

Three Prose Poems

FAMILY MOTTO

A terrible tribe. Break before bend is their motto. So they break and then mend stiffer and stronger than ever before. Locked into a tower of bone and stone. Immobile, frozen stiff, a living death. Lord, let me bend to this shifting life. Melt, merge, release, let go. Grow.

INVOCATION

Standing on the path between river and canal, in a springtime watercolor world, I decide to make a memory. The exact way the river bends, flash of sunlight making water opaque, green leaves transparent. Voluptuous smell of river mud. Acrid scent of sun-warmed stone. Unpaintable, unforgettable. I cannot paint the breeze that cools the damp hair on my neck, the feel of your hand in mine. Feeling of oneness with this bounty of earth, air, sky, and you. Unpaintable. Unforgettable.

THE WALTZ

One night there was a party, large and fancy, a dance, a ball, and I was there wearing a black tulle off-the-shoulder dress and I was asked to waltz, the Viennese Waltz, to save that one dance for him. Who? I don't know now, the waltzer, that's who. And we danced around the high-ceiling room through the door and into the hall and the next room and everyone stopped, the dancers, the drinkers, the talkers, all stopped and watched us waltz and we were ourselves and the music and the dance and the absolute center of the universe . . . that night.

Ruby Slippers

On the radio, Oceans 400,
every Judy Garland song
ends with applause.

Then I am off
on my personal wave
of memory and
my only disappointment
in Judy Garland.

I was a little girl
when "The Wizard of Oz"
was first screened.
A real little girl,
flat-chested, waistless,
scabby kneed and freckled.

There was Judy,
pigtailed, doe-eyed,
and definitely in possession
of a chest, as I would
have said then.

Now the word is boob.
Try as they might
there is no disguising it.
Judy, that is to say, Dorothy
—Dorothy with boobs.

She could sing, my, yes,
and dance, and cry
quite prettily, but
she was simply too old
to play Dorothy.

I had read the
book and knew
that Dorothy was
a little girl like me.
Yes, that was it:
I should have
played Dorothy.

Time passes, linear,
circular, and now
I have granddaughters
who pose perfectly
beside any handy fence
and burst into
"Somewhere over the rainbow."

The Emerald City lives.
We are there
in our ruby slippers.

Love, Love, Love

We sit beside the river bank
the greenest grass that ever grew
underneath our lazing asses.

Your perfect, agile fingers
work to make a willow whistle.
River water, brown, flecked
with gold, a large reflection
of your eyes, that dance
into mine and tantalize.

Drunk on smell of new-mown
hay, or is it honeysuckle?
I am in love, love, love.

Privileged

I lie awake at three a.m.
listening to an echoed
tangle of laughter.
Tee-hees, titters, chuckles, and
guffaws; trills, bellows,
hiccups, and roars.
A recent event
engraved on my ear.

Fresca's fiftieth birthday
and all the clan
gathered to celebrate.
Which we have done
with wine and song
and laughter.

I am the matriarch.
I have changed the
diapers of twelve of
those here, which
means they have
all, also, been
belly-wuffled by me.

Starting this laughter.
Starting them.

Starting myself,
this matriarch, a stranger
to the girl who lives
inside this old lady shell.
The one who takes
off her glasses when
she looks in the mirror.

This girl who still might
walk across the Brooklyn bridge,
go up in a hot air balloon.
Play another part,
play in the garden,
play in the kitchen,
play at the desk,

serene in the knowledge
that I will never get
past the first fifteen
pages of "Remembrance
of Times Past."
Happily pretend that
I have read "Moby Dick," and
still think I might have a shot
at Dante's "Inferno"
before I go elsewhere.

Who knows, maybe join the
ones who changed my diapers,
sang to me, read to me.
Then again, be a guardian angel
to those who are yet to come.

This moment this woman is
a great golden lioness
who grabs the rolling
ball of now and holds
it softly in her paws.

Fast Fall

Have I ever really
been in love?
Wedded twice
and bedded
more times than I
care to count, but
been in love?

Why yes, I believe
I have.
Skidded round the
corner and slipped,
fallen in that place:
Love.

Brief brightness I recall.
Brilliance too strong to last
and then another kind of fall.
Into sorrow, out of love.
into the dark of fear,
the long road back
to simply loving.

Never out of love
with life.
Never long in love
with love.

On Acting

Everyone thinks that an actor
does it for the applause,
the love, the possible fame.
They are right.

Sort of. But that is not
the whole story, there
is more than that.

Actors get to be
all of their selves.
The mean, angry persona
can strut and fret

her little hour
upon the stage
without alienating
her most near and dear
entirely.

Can lose herself
not unlike Zen.
But best of all
are the times when

all the cast are
playing so well,
no net needed,
that they are part
of something bigger.
Clean into another
character, soul.

It is like being
in a huddle of puppies.
The litter adjusting
to one another.

Keeping warm, close.
Perfect trust.
Rare and wonderful.

Whensday

Before I acquired so many labels
before rebel, flirt, mother, actress, wife,
but not before sister, daughter, child,
wild child, shy child.

Before most of the labels
and all of the masks,
but not before love, hate
and friendship.

Back then

when I stood at
the top of the stairs,
looked through the
window of the broad
landing

and saw

the whole world before me,
the curve of the globe,
the land and sea and
all the creatures
thereon.

Saw them and knew them
for what they were
and so knowing
knew
who I was.

Then came life,
the long forgetting.
Three score and ten years
and now I almost remember.

Chooseday, Whensday, Someday,
it may come back again.

Ambition

What do I want to be.
    Not
what do I want to have.

I have wanted to have
    it all:
house, car, happy family
appreciation, applause.

    But wait.

I have wanted to be—
an actor, a mother,
a singer, a writer,
a lover, beloved.

And some of this
being and having
I have been and had.

Been and had
gone and done.

Shouting nearly over,
    still I want.

Having has faded
but Being rises,
clear definite, real.
I want to be
grace.

Mine

Here is my truth.
An elastic truth
that is ever changing
and always.

My grain of sand
among all the
other grains.
Without which
there would be
no beach.

The beach being
God.
The whole truth.

God who is Allah
or Jehovah
or simply,
the powers that be.

God who has no name,
whose name is
secret and manifold,
sacred and profane,
everywhere and nowhere.

The whole truth
to which
my truth aspires.

9-11 **911

Emergency—Mayday
September day
Blue and gold
Gone black with
fire, smoke, ashes.
Who are they?
What do they want?
Terrorists want terror
they want fear.
Eyes blinded with grief
Let's not be blinded with fear.
In the face of evil
Oh Souls, let us
be brave enough to love.

Thanksgiving

The trouble with age is—
Oh, hell, the troubles
with age are . . . simple.

That maple seedling you
didn't see, neglected to
pull, has grown into

a sapling over the
garage, too close,
and will make even

more shade than
there is now.
If you could

you would cut
down that sapling,
a simple job

if you had done
it twenty years ago.
Now you need

to find a kid,
a younger person
to help you out.

They're willing enough,
work for cash or love,
or both . . . but . . .

Heaven help them.
They are so busy
pulling out their own weeds

that they forget.
You do too.
The sapling grows

into a tree. You look
out the window
see a small brown bird
perched on a limb,
think of starting
a new shade garden.

Surprise Compromise

Listen: I lay in the sun
warm to the very core
of my being
a big bubble-crusted
golden pie
smoking cigarettes
and eating empty
calories.

Listen: fragile lace bones
and polka-dotted
pleated skin
are not the style
statement I had in
mind for my old age.

Listen: I didn't have
a plan
and this is what
comes of it
any old rag
hauled from the closet
will have to do.

Trust

I should have kept my eyes peeled.
Not me, floating down the
river Nile.

Eyes in rose colored glasses.
Heart wrapped in gauze
but open still.

Now my peeled eyes
leak endless tears.

My closed heart has
turned to stone.

How to go on?
Is it possible

to have peeled eyes
and an open heart?

Hug from Hell

Born eager to embrace the world
and hold close every delicious molecule,

I have received some spectacular
dents and cuts and bruises

along with the honey and wine,
dog slobber, child snot, wind clasp.

The latest embrace that
broke bones of lace

left ribs and back
crunched and displaced

has not squelched
my hungry hug.

Generations

I called my grandmother,
the one who lived
in another state,

the one I knew less well,
to congratulate her on
her ninety-second birthday.

"What for?" she said
"I have outlived
everyone who
knew me when
I was young.
I have lived too long."

What could I say?
I protested that
last sentence.

Now that I am
two decades away
or closer to, ninety-two.

I am sad and glad
That I didn't say
"For us."

Start

Presented with the Bowl of Morning
I put my dreams around my shoulders,

stuff my face into the pillow,
pretend that I will stay in bed.

The need to pee interferes with
my plans, and eyes again open

see an expanse of perfect blue
punctuated with one white seagull.

Crawling out of bed, I accept
the challenge of beauty,
the need to pee,
    another day.

Travel Lite

The little cares that fretted me,
I lost them yesterday,
I packed them in my suitcase
left them at the bus stop
and took the bus away.

Good-bye, old cares, I called
as the bus got up to speed.
Maybe someone will find you,
give you the attention you need.

As for me, I'm sailing
along the smooth highway.
No more need for baggage.
This is another day.

Now I'm sailing down the road
eyes ahead to wide expanse.
Nothing like a little trip
to bring your life romance.

No extraordinary measures

I will say yes
　　to life
until life says
　　no to me.
Vain, silly, proud
　　I may be
and that is
　　being kind.
Still and yet
　　relish
must count
　　for something.
I will say yes
　　to life
until death comes
　　with final
notice.
　　Then, only then
I most
　　certainly wish
to say yes
　　to death.
Be let go
　　not held back
by meddling medics
　　or near and dear.
Allowed to embrace
　　death as I have
life, with grace.

In Progress

Before I go, I would like to say
how much I've enjoyed the party.
I don't know where I'm going
or how long I will be gone,
but keep the party going,
taste all the dishes
even the bitter ones, it's
those that increase the value of sweets.
And even though I seem to be gone
don't be absolutely sure.
I was ever and ever a party girl.

In case I don't remember,
remember for me.
Even the nights we drank too much,
committed *in vino veritas*
and awoke next day with
a dreadful head.
I would like to remember
the feel of your hand in
mine, mine in yours,
the feel of sunlight
and rain, and bare feet.
The feet I came to
the party with, and I shall
kick off my shoes
when I go. Always

wanting to know the
stories that come from
the sole, the soul.
The softness of moss,
the agony of stones,
the pleasant grit of sand,
the balm of water
after the hot coals,
the marvel of dewy grass,
the sting of snow.
Even if I am not at the party
Feel them for me.

And sniff for me, please.
Pines, sour milk, apple blossom,
coffee, cigarettes, and babies.
The burning of soft coal
that builds a city in interior view.
Lemons and lavender for
the warmth of the sun.
The many smells of earth
in garden, forest and swamp.

Then there's the moon, the fog
the sweet, soft air
after a summer storm.
This list is too long.
Someone will start a roll
of drums, to get me
off the podium
before I start thanking
the family cat, and the
dog whose name is
God spelled backwards
all my friends, my babies
and their babies and all
those who knew, and especially
those who didn't,
how important they were.
It wouldn't have
been a party without
them, without you.

I was always and ever
a party girl, but if
time has come to go
as sooner or later it will,
then pause just a little,
sing a song, dance barefooted,

breathe deep the air.
Clean your plate,
so that if by chance
I should return
as beetle, or queen,
or coffee urn,
I'll find you there
at the party.